This Journal Belongs to :

Made in the USA
Coppell, TX
11 July 2022

79839162R00057